How I Feel

I Feel Happy

By Connor Stratton

level
2
little blue
readers

www.littlebluehousebooks.com

Little Blue House is distributed by North Star Editions:
sales@northstareditions.com | 888-417-0195

Produced for Little Blue House by Red Line Editorial.

Photographs ©: Shutterstock Images, cover, 4, 6–7, 9, 10–11, 14–15, 17, 18, 20–21, 23, 24 (top left), 24 (top right), 24 (bottom left), 24 (bottom right); iStockphoto, 12

Library of Congress Control Number: 2020913843

ISBN
978-1-64619-297-7 (hardcover)
978-1-64619-315-8 (paperback)
978-1-64619-351-6 (ebook pdf)
978-1-64619-333-2 (hosted ebook)

Printed in the United States of America
Mankato, MN
012021

About the Author

Connor Stratton enjoys writing books for children and watching movies, such as *Inside Out*. He's always trying to understand his feelings better. He lives in Minnesota.

Table of Contents

Why I'm Happy

I am playing on the slide.

That's why I'm happy.

I am eating a treat.

That's why I'm happy.

I am opening a present.

That's why I'm happy.

I made a friend.

That's why I'm happy.

family

Happy People

I feel happy at different times. I feel happy with my family.

I feel happy with
my friends.

friends

I even feel happy
by myself.

What I Do

I feel happy.

I jump in the air.

I feel happy.

I hug my friend.

I feel happy.

I have a big smile.

Glossary

present

smile

slide

treats

Index